THE BATTLE OF STALINGRAD

The First Defeat of the German Wehrmacht

Written by Jérémy Rocteur
In collaboration with Laure Delacroix
Translated by Carly Probert

History 50MINUTES.com

THE BATTLE OF STALINGRAD

KEY INFORMATION

- **When:** 23 August 1942 – 2 February 1943
- **Where:** At Stalingrad (now Volgograd, Russia)
- **Context:** World War II (1939-1945)
- **Belligerents:** The Soviet Union against the Third Reich
- **Commanders and leaders:**
  - Friedrich Wilhelm Ernst Paulus, German Marshal (1890-1957)
  - Vasily Ivanovich Chuikov, Russian General (1900-1982)
- **Outcome:** Russian victory
- **Victims:**
  - Russian camp: approximately 500 000 dead or missing civilians and soldiers
  - German camp: approximately 150 000 dead or missing and more than 110 000 taken prisoner

INTRODUCTION

A turning point of the Second World War, the Battle of Stalingrad introduced a new form of confrontation: close combat in urban areas.

In the summer of 1942, the goal of the German leader Adolf Hitler (1889-1945) on the Eastern Front was to capture the Caucasus and its oil in order to deliver a fatal blow to the Soviet economy. Starting from the Kharkov region (in eastern Ukraine), the German troops were divided in two: the first armed group headed south, to the Caucasus and its oil fields, while the 6ᵗʰ army of General Friedrich Wilhelm Ernst Paulus went to Stalingrad, situated along the Volga (Russian river).

Although fighting first broke out on 17 July in the city's surrounding areas, the attack did not actually begin until 23 August 1942. Through this initiative, Adolf Hitler aimed to protect the northern flank of the troops advancing towards the Caucasus, cut the Russian communication lines and ultimately use them to head back towards Moscow.

The city's name quickly became a symbol and the scene of a fierce battle between the Germans and the Russians. The street fights that ensued there took place on an unprece-dented scale and the battle was slowly becoming a personal matter for the Führer, who insisted on continuing the offensive.

In a ruined city, under the command of General Vasily Ivanovich Chuikov, the Red Army managed to resist and en-circle the 6ᵗʰ German army, which surrendered in February 1943. For the first time since the beginning of the war, the German troops had been defeated and were forced to capitulate.

POLITICAL AND SOCIAL CONTEXT

THE ORIGINS OF THE CONFLICT

The Second World War began on 1 September 1939 with the invasion of Poland by the German army, forcing Britain and France, the guarantor countries of Polish independence, to mobilize against Germany. The German leader faced these two countries on the Western Front, without being attacked from behind, thanks to the non-aggression pact that had been concluded with the main power in the east, the USSR, which participated in the Polish defeat in September 1939.

Signed in August of the same year, the pact known as the "Molotov-Ribbentrop Pact", named after the German and Soviet ministers of foreign affairs at the time, was based on a common desire for the destruction of the Polish state. Organizing the dismemberment of the country after its defeat, the agreement also defined the areas of German and Soviet influence in Eastern Europe.

As for Britain and France, they were powerless against these attacks governed by new military tactics: *Blitzkrieg*, or "lightning war".

GOOD TO KNOW

The watchword of *Blitzkrieg* means to move forward as quickly as possible into enemy terrain using a motorized army and to carry out an extensive encirclement of enemy troops for a quick victory. With the unfailing support of the *Luftwaffe* (German air force), this method ensured the success of the German army until the summer of 1942.

Thanks to this new method of attack, the German troops won many victories in the first year of the war, so much so that in the spring of 1941, the majority of Europe was under its domination. Britain remained the only country on the continent that was fully able to continue fighting against it. Although the British did not have the slightest chance of emerging victorious, they refused all peace offers, making the Führer believe that they carried on resisting because they hoped for the intervention of a European ally. With the continent almost entirely under his control, Hitler deduced that this ally could only have been the Soviet Union. The defeat of the British Empire was therefore only possible after a defeat of the USSR, according to the Führer's logic.

This reason was accompanied by an economic factor. The German Empire that Adolf Hitler was building through his policies of conquest and annexation had to be autonomous in terms of food and raw materials. Consequently, in order to achieve this, he had to acquire large territories, which were abundant in the Soviet Union. It therefore seemed necessary to invade the USSR by opening a new front in the east.

THE INVASION OF THE SOVIET UNION

More than just a surprise attack, the German invasion of the Soviet Union was primarily a dramatic turnaround of alliances. Before launching the hostilities, Germany ensured new secret coalitions with Finland, Hungary, Romania and Italy in order to gain their support and on 22 June 1941, Operation Barbarossa was launched. More than five million people – two thirds of the German forces – participated in the state attack. The attack aimed to be quick and decisive and to defeat the Soviet Union in just four months.

However, in December 1941, after taking control of the Baltic States, Belarus and most of Ukraine, the German troops failed when they reached the gates of Moscow. Despite the appalling losses suffered by the Red Army, the Soviet troops managed to strike back. The Germans were forced to retreat, sometimes by more than 250 kilometers, but they managed to maintain strategic positions that the Russians simply bypassed.

THE SOVIET UNION ON THE BRINK

The German occupation of almost half of the Soviet European territories – or the richest and most populated part of Russia – plunged the state into crisis and involved serious consequences for the economy. Between 1941 and 1942:

- its workforce fell from 87 million to 55 million inhabitants;
- its grain production fell from 95 to 30 million tons;

- its motor vehicle production was reduced by two thirds.

The Red Army, severely undermined by the German invasion, painfully tried to rebuild itself. However, with the move of more than 2 000 factories that were now out of reach for the Germans, production was able to gradually recommence.

Despite this, Joseph Stalin (1878-1953) decided to attack from May 1942. Still motivated by the success of the counter-attack in December 1941, the Soviet leader primarily sought to harass the German army to prevent it from recovering its strength. A series of attacks was then organized along the front to consolidate the successes gained, at the cost of many lives, during the previous winter. But these attacks, which were ill-prepared, quickly led to new defeats in the Soviet camp, the most spectacular of which was the Battle of Kharkov (12 May 1942), where hundreds of thousands of Russian soldiers were taken prisoner. Learning from this new disaster, Joseph Stalin decided to authorize the retreat of his troops and to not execute the defeated generals as he had done before. This realization would prove beneficial to the fighting that would soon take place in the Caucasus.

GOOD TO KNOW

The fourth industrial center of the USSR, Kharkov is a city in Eastern Ukraine, occupied by the Germans from October 1941. The Soviets were determined to recapture it and an attack led by Semyon Konstantinovich Timoshenko (Soviet Marshal, 1895-1970) was planned for the beginning of May 1942. His plan was simple: trapping the opponent with two army groups. However, the opposing forces were underestimated and the Soviets chose to attack at the strongest point of the German front. The assault was launched on 12 May. Taken by surprise, the Germans were forced to lose ground. However, noting that the Russians had piled up their defenses in Kharkov, the German generals decided to attack them from the rear and re-joined behind the forces of Semyon Konstantinovich Timoshenko. They then managed to take 240 000 prisoners and destroyed 1 200 tanks, making the Battle of Kharkov one of the worst disasters suffered by the Russian Army during the Second World War.

Moreover, the Soviet leader understood that he could not wage a war without outside help. Therefore, Britain and the United States came to its rescue by providing the food, oil, gunpowder and explosives needed for the war effort in 1941.

CONTROL OF THE CAUCASUS OIL

Although at the height of its power, the *Wehrmacht* (German army) was unable to bend the Soviet Union in 1941. Indeed, the *Blitzkrieg* tactics were not adapted to a territory as vast as that of the USSR and they gradually revealed their limits. Now with fewer resources while the Eastern Front stretched for hundreds of kilometers, the German generals, under the direction of Adolf Hitler, decided to focus their efforts on the Caucasus and its oil.

Of utmost importance during the war, this liquid gold allowed the Germans to ensure the smooth running of their many motorized divisions and thus continue their advance, while making it inaccessible to the Russians.

The operation developed in this way – which carried the name "Blau" – was therefore intended to strike a fatal blow, not only to the Soviet economy, but also to the Red Army, by conducting a large encirclement of hundreds of thousands of Russians soldiers. To do this, the Germans were forced to leave the region of Kharkov and divide: the mission of the first group was to travel to the South Caucasus and its oil fields, while the 6th army of General Friedrich Wilhelm Ernst Paulus headed towards Stalingrad, a true pivoting point between Russia and the Caucasus.

Located on the western banks of the Volga, the city was on a vital axis for Russia, since it was through there that communications passed between the north and south of the country, as well as foreign aid.

However, its conquest was not a priority objective of Operation Blau. For the Germans, the aim in September was to destroy the factories there and interrupt the river traffic. But, following the failure of the Caucasus campaign and the stubborn resistance shown by the Soviet troops, Adolf Hitler insisted on taking control of the city and refused to compromise, despite the losses incurred.

COMMANDERS AND LEADERS

VASILY IVANOVICH CHUIKOV, RUSSIAN GENERAL

Coming from a modest background, Vasily Ivanovich Chuikov was born in 1900 in the Russian province of Tula. He joined the Red Army in 1918 and participated in the Second World War. However, when the conflict broke out, he was sent to China to help the Chinese statesman Chiang Kai-shek (1887-1975) in his war against Japan.

On 12 September 1942, the Soviet High Command appointed him as head of the 62nd army responsible for defending the city of Stalingrad. Although his mission seemed unattainable, he directed the 20 000 men under his command with a firm hand and set up an improvised defense. His mission was complex: he had to hold the city until the arrival of reinforcements and to achieve this he was prepared to sacrifice his men in order to save time. Reputed to be one of the most ruthless Russian generals, he terrorized his commanders by categorically denying them any retreat and did not hesitate to summarily execute deserters. Therefore, he had more than 10 000 soldiers executed during the battle on the grounds of treason.

While defending the city, Vasily Ivanovich Chuikov sought to reduce the main force of the Germans: their aviation. He also knew of a few weak points, which he played on to his advantage. Thus, he knew that his opponents hated close combat and therefore did everything possible to create it.

He also decided to use the main obstacle encountered by Hitler's army in Stalingrad: the ruins of the city. He lured the German troops to the ruins and immobilized them there, consequently limiting the opportunity for the intervention of the *Luftwaffe* in Stalingrad. In addition, he moved all of his heavy artillery to the eastern bank of the Volga to support the defense of the city.

Once the troops of Friedrich Wilhelm Ernst Paulus were trapped in the city, the Russian general's objective was to increase large-scale attacks by using the fortified positions, towards which the German troops rushed, only to find themselves divided and facing Soviet tanks that were half-buried in the rubble. He also revolutionized urban combat, making it a real art, and was the source of what the Germans called *Rattenkrieg* ("war of rats"), a mode of close combat in urban areas which completely disoriented the soldiers of the Third Reich.

Despite their progression, the Germans failed to take control of the city. The task was even more complex as Vasily Ivanovich Chuikov constantly moved his headquarters. He managed to hold the city thanks to reinforcements that constantly arrived from the other bank of the river until the launch of the Russian counter-attack at the end of November.

Due to his audacity and ardor in battle, he was made a Hero of the Soviet Union, the highest award under the Stalinist regime. After this victory, he participated in the final attack on Berlin in April 1945 and obtained the rank of marshal at the end of the war.

After holding the position of Deputy Minister of Defense, he died in 1982 and was laid to rest at the foot of the statue of The Motherland on Mamayev Hill in Volgograd, where the memorial of the Battle of Stalingrad is located.

FRIEDRICH WILHELM ERNST PAULUS, GERMAN MARSHAL

Hailing from a family of petty officials of the German region of Hesse, Friedrich Wilhelm Ernst Paulus participated in the First World War (1914-1918), from which he emerged with the rank of captain. He also fought during World War II, taking part in the invasion of Poland in 1939 and the campaign in France.

GOOD TO KNOW

After the German invasion of Belgium, the Netherlands and France in May 1940, the French army retreated and installed a defense line on the Aisne and the Somme, where the Battle of France was held. With a German army that was three times the size of that of the French, with no air support and sorely lacking in heavy weapons, the French were in bad shape. Still, they managed to slow the progression of the Germans. A new attack was then launched on 9 June in Champagne. The French forces were attacked on several fronts and collapsed. The capital being threatened, the government of Paul Reynaud (1878-1966) hastily left Paris for Bordeaux. The Battle of France was lost.

He later held a strategist position in the high command of the German army, and participated in the planning of the invasion of the USSR. While he never commanded a regiment or division, he was catapulted to the head of the 6th Army in January 1942, following the death of his predecessor.

Emerging from the Battle of Kharkov victorious in May, on 14 August of the same year he received the mission to take the city of Stalingrad with the 6th Army, where it would face fierce resistance from the Red Army.

A meticulous strategist, the German marshal felt more comfortable behind a desk than on the front. He therefore revealed himself to be completely baffled in the face of the *Rattenkrieg* carried out by his opponent. Blindly respecting the chain of command, he scrupulously obeyed the orders of Adolf Hitler and constantly repeated assaults on the Soviet positions to satisfy the obsession of his leader. It was also on the orders of the Führer that he clung to the city, rather than trying to free himself from the Russian encirclement.

At the end of January 1943, Adolf Hitler appointed him marshal in the hope that, through the dignity of the rank – the highest in the German army -, he would choose to commit suicide rather than be captured and thus be dishonored. Yet although he appeared cold through his manners and his scrawny physique, Friedrich Wilhelm Ernst Paulus was sincerely concerned for the welfare of his soldiers. He knew that his troops could not continue fighting and that his situation was hopeless. Therefore, he decided to surrender on 31 January 1943, the day after his promotion, and was captured.

From July 1944, while he remained in custody, he served in the Soviet propaganda by frequently addressing the German armies stationed on the Eastern Front by radio, in order to convince them to surrender. He was released a few years later after testifying against the Nazi leaders in the Nuremberg trials (1945-1946) and decided to retire in Dresden, where he died in 1957.

ANALYSIS OF THE BATTLE

THE *WEHRMACHT* AT THE GATES OF THE CITY

After separating from the troops that were supposed to take the Caucasus, the 6th Army of Friedrich Wilhelm Ernst Paulus reached the gates of the city in late August. Vastly superior in numbers and equipment, there was confidence in the German ranks. Indeed, the general had about 300 000 men and formidable air support, whereas the Russian troops stationed in the city had only 25 000 men. For the Germans, the capture of the city would only take a few days and the general estimated the fighting to last no more than a week and a half.

On 23 August, the battle began with a massive bombardment of the city by the *Luftwaffe*, in order to terrorize the population and break the morale of the defenders. The operation was a success and there were no fewer than 40 000 deaths among the population. To fill the losses incurred in the Russian army, civilians were forcibly incorporated. Women and children were also enlisted. Soon, hundreds of bombs were dropped, transforming the city into a vast field of ruins that the Russians would later use against the Germans.

Stalingrad partly destroyed by German bombings.

On 12 September, while the German army advanced in the suburbs of Stalingrad, General Vasily Ivanovich Chuikov was appointed head of the defenders of the city. Without anti-aircraft guns to neutralize the deadly air raids from the German aviation and with only 20 000 men, whose morale was extremely low, the situation seemed hopeless. The defenders of the city had to try to exhaust the Germans until reinforcements arrived. He decided to use a method that was revolutionary for its time: close combat in urban areas.

THE RESISTANCE OF THE RED ARMY

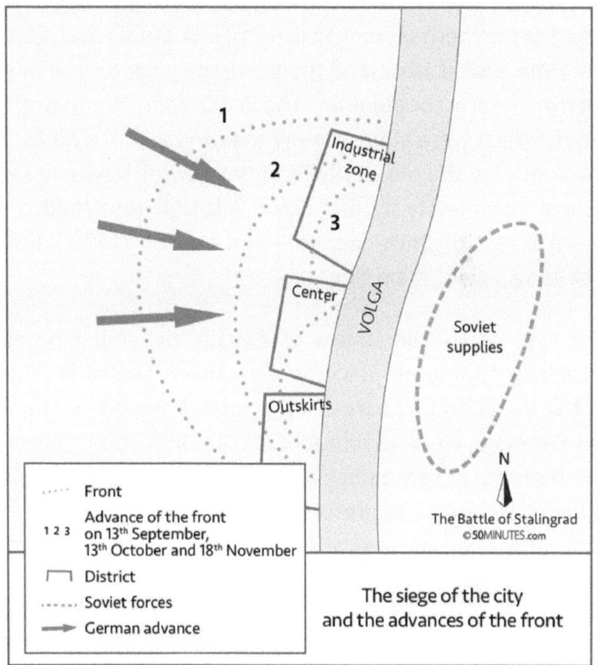

Stalingrad was a very narrow city, stretching along the west bank of the Volga. Therefore, the Germans' favorite tactic of encircling their opponents could not be implemented, as the river was too wide. Only one solution remained: a massive frontal attack on the city.

On 13 September, the German soldiers set out to attack the

center of Stalingrad. To prevent any overflow attempts by the flanks, Vasily Ivanovich Chuikov first intended to firmly secure his troops in the northern and southern ends of the city. The northern sector consisted of industrial areas, which were the easiest to defend thanks to the gigantic buildings, such as the tractor plant and the *Red October* metallurgical plant, which were almost impregnable resistance poles. To the south lay the old city built of wood, which was already almost completely burned down. All that remained of it was a forest of brick chimneys and a few solid buildings, including a giant grain silo.

The fate of the defenders essentially depended on the refuelling that took place at night from the other bank of the Volga and by barges, and throughout the battle, as the Germans were unable to cut the connection. Thus, in the months of September and October, 100 000 Russian soldiers arrived as reinforcements in Stalingrad. However, communications were severed when winter arrived, making navigation on the river impossible.

As for the Germans, they advanced into the city in small infantry groups supported by tanks, which proved particularly vulnerable in the street fighting. With the upper floors of buildings being out of shooting range, the Russian infantry took advantage of this to attack the weaknesses of their opponents: the roof and the engine compartment.

German soldiers make their way through Stalingrad ruins

Furthermore, Vasily Ivanovich Chuikov took care to develop the techniques of urban combat with his men, favoring several tactics which involved:

- seeking close combat;
- attacking at night;
- harassing the German troops with elite gunmen during the day;
- transforming homes and factories into fortresses.

To do this, the defenders of the city edged quietly closer to the positions of the enemy to surprise them during the attack and, during the night, they moved through the sewers to take over the positions lost during the day. Therefore, when the Germans finally managed to siege a building and attack, the Russians took advantage of the night to resume their former positions. The battle was exhausting for both sides, but it was a living hell for the soldiers of Friedrich Wilhelm Ernst Paulus: this "war of rats" undermined the morale of the attackers. The progression of the 6th Army was therefore very slow, because the advance could no longer be measured in kilometers, but in meters. Fighting took place all over the city. The determination and courage shown by the Russian soldiers surprised the Germans and the Soviet artillery, on the eastern bank of the Volga, constantly harassed them.

Snipers entering a ruined house.

Despite the harshness of the battle, the Red Army did not abandon, which can be explained by several factors:

- Fear of being captured. During the war on the Eastern Front, the German army killed over 4 million Soviet prisoners of war, mostly by starving them. The fighters knew of this and thus desperately fought so as not to fall into the hands of the enemy.

- The power of Russian patriotism. Political propaganda opposing communism to fascism was abandoned in favor of the defense of "Mother Russia", a true personification of the state which appeared on all patriotic posters.
- The police and political leadership. Declared under siege from 25 August, martial law reigned in Stalingrad where repression played an important role in the clashes. The Russian fighters were tightly supervised by political commissars who suppressed any attempts at surrender or retreat with execution.
- Mass participation in the defense of the city. Many workers, women and adolescents took part in the defense of Stalingrad and fought to defend their homes.
- The power of Soviet propaganda. Russia conveyed the image of a final ditch, according to which Stalingrad was the final obstacle between German barbarism and Russian soil. Russia must fight, or be destroyed.

Despite their heroic resistance, the perimeter defended by the Russians gradually reduced. The Germans were gaining ground and managed to take the southern sector. However, after more than a month of fierce fighting, the city, now more than 90% destroyed, still had not fallen, which was hardly pleasing to the Führer. In addition, the first army group in the south was also blocked in its offensive to take the Caucasus, so the success of the Battle of Stalingrad depended entirely on the campaign of 1942. Given the urgency of the situation, Adolf Hitler decided to take over control of the army on the Eastern Front himself. While the reserve forces were no longer sufficient to provide relief, he persisted and forced the 4th Army, although exhausted, to continue the attack.

Russian infantry in rubble of Stalingrad.

By early November, the Germans controlled more than nine tenths of the city, but the last Russian defenders were still refusing to surrender. The situation was even more critical as the winter and the cold threatened the troops. With temperatures falling below -20°C, the Volga turned into huge blocks of ice and became unfit for navigation. Deprived of their main supply route, the situation of the defenders seemed hopeless.

THE RUSSIAN COUNTER-ATTACK

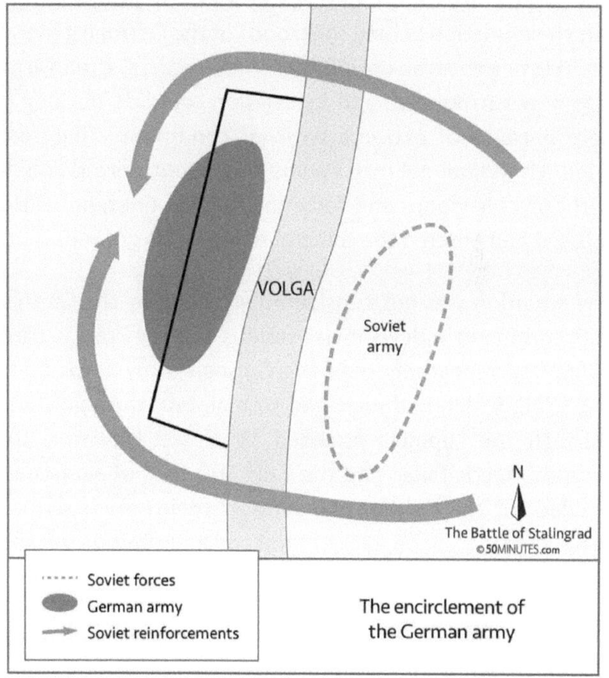

The Battle of Stalingrad
© 50MINUTES.com

The encirclement of
the German army

From October, the Russian troops that had been retreating since the beginning of Operation Blau were preparing for a broad counter-offensive, which would target the most vulnerable spot of the army of Friedrich Wilhelm Ernst Paulus, namely its flanks.

On 19 November, part of the group attacked and the northern flank of the 6th Army was pushed back, while a second offensive was launched on the 20 November, this time in the south. The following day, the Russian troops carried out their junction behind the troops of the German general, thus closing the trap on 260 000 soldiers: the German army was now surrounded, and its aviation could do nothing to help because of extreme weather conditions. Therefore, Friedrich Wilhelm Ernst Paulus requested permission to withdraw his troops and force the Russian lines, but Hitler refused and ordered the General to stand his ground.

The situation was not considered alarming by the German high command. Indeed, it was serious, but the Russian campaign had repeatedly seen the German army corps being encircled, which had managed to maintain their positions through the supplies provided by airlift. However, this time the tactic failed and the daily 500 tons of equipment needed for the Germans to support their efforts did not reach the front. Soon, lack of food and ammunition became a problem.

On 12 December, a ground attempt was launched to free the encircled army. A simultaneous attack with General Friedrich Wilhelm Ernst Paulus could have released the encirclement of the 6th Army, but, loyal to the orders of the Führer to retain every bit of land acquired, he refused to reduce his lines and did not move. So, faced with the pressure from the Soviets, the operation failed and the forces of the German army continued to decline.

The first days of 1943 saw the 6th Army rapidly sink. Beset by permanent firing and the incessant attacks of the Russians, who gradually reduced their pocket of resistance, the German soldiers were cold and hungry. On 26 January, the troops were again divided in two by a new Russian attack. Knowing that the situation was desperate, the German general requested permission to capitulate, but this was formally denied. To prevent him from surrendering and to push him towards suicide, Adolf Hitler appointed him marshal on 30 January. However, the next day Friedrich Wilhelm Ernst Paulus surrendered and signed the capitulation of his army. A few days later, the last German soldiers stopped fighting: the surrender was complete.

Surrender of Friedrich Wilhelm Ernst Paulus.

The toll was heavy for both armies:

• in the Soviet camp, there were 500 000 dead or missing

civilians and soldiers;

- in the German camp, there were 150 000 dead or missing and more than 110 000 prisoners.

Although the Russian losses were greater, the victory was total for the Red Army, which not only managed to defeat a German army, but also forced it to surrender.

THE GERMAN ERRORS

At the Battle of Stalingrad, the troops of General Vasily Ivanovich Chuikov performed a feat by taking down one of the best German armies. To achieve this, the Russians took advantage of some German errors, such as:

- The late attack on Stalingrad by the 6th Army. Indeed, the city could have been taken as soon as July, when it was not being defended. However, priority was given to operations taking place in the Caucasus, which slowed the advance of Friedrich Wilhelm Ernst Paulus.
- The lack of reserve troops. Once urban combat had been initiated, the German general suffered from not being able to rely on reserves that could relieve the exhausted troops.
- The misjudgment of the Russian troops. German strategists were convinced that the Russians were using their last resources on the defense of the city. The massive counter-attack in November was therefore a surprise.
- The successive errors of German intelligence services. They were unable to provide accurate information of the potential and the intentions of the Soviet troops. These

misunderstandings in turn led to significant mistakes of appreciation on the part of the German generals.

However, other reasons may explain the disastrous outcome of the battle:

- The failure of the airlift. Besides the bad weather of the winter of 1942, the establishment and organization of the airlift was slow. The aerodromes responsible for ensuring liaison with Stalingrad did not have adequate airstrips to support air traffic of this magnitude. Finally, the Soviet fighter aviation had grown significantly since the summer. The failure of the airlift marks the beginning of the decline of German supremacy in the air.
- The obstinacy of Adolf Hitler. By stubbornly wanting to take Stalingrad, whatever the cost, and leaving this ruined city to the troops of General Friedrich Wilhelm Ernst Paulus, the main person responsible for the destruction of the 6th Army was the Führer. Unlike Joseph Stalin, he no longer listened to his generals. However, he made the conflict personal and led the operations in the Caucasus primarily for psychological reasons: his power over the German people had been based on his frequent victories since the outbreak of the Second World War. But since the failure of Operation Barbarossa, the capture of the Caucasus and the recent setbacks of the *Afrikakorps* at the gates of Cairo in November 1941, doubts were being casted among the German population. Adolf Hitler therefore needed a victory at Stalingrad.

The *Afrikakorps* was a German contingent sent to North Africa in early 1941 to ensure control over the southern Mediterranean. Under the command of General Erwin Rommel (1891-1944), this elite corps won many successes against the British. The most spectacular of these was the capture of the Libyan port of Tobruk in June 1942, which appeared to open the doors to the Suez Canal for the German troops.

However, they suffered a decisive defeat in November 1942 at the battle of El Alamein in Egypt, where they were repelled by the British. This failure marked the beginning of the retreat of the *Afrikakorps* and the end of the German presence in North Africa.

REPERCUSSIONS OF THE BATTLE

THE TOTAL FAILURE OF THE GERMAN CAMPAIGN

The outcome of the 1942 campaign was catastrophic for Adolf Hitler. Its main objective, which was to take possession of the Caucasus and its oil fields, was not achieved. Even worse, one of his most powerful armies was annihilated. Of the 300 000 men in the 6th Army in the summer of 1942, nearly 280 000 were put out of action after the battle.

Although their losses were much heavier, the Russians had the ability to replace their personnel and their equipment. On the contrary, Germany, having been at war for three years, was in a deep crisis and no longer had any reserves on the Eastern Front, the deadliest of the war. Over three quarters of the battles that occurred during the war took place there and more than 90% of the German losses during WWII happened there.

The defeat of Stalingrad did not mark the end of the *Wehrmacht*. The Russians pushed their counter-attack much too far and suffered further setbacks in the spring of 1943. Despite the loss of the 6th Army, the Germans had returned to the positions they held at the beginning of Operation Blau by March. During the summer, the German army launched a final attempt to regain the upper hand on the Eastern Front during the Battle of Kursk (Russia), which resulted in a further German defeat that was even more disastrous than that experienced in Stalingrad. The best divisions of the German tanks were destroyed. Kursk marked the permanent loss of the German offensive in Russia. The Germans now realized that a total victory over the Red Army was no longer possible and adopted a defensive position until the ultimate defeat of the Third Reich in Berlin in spring 1945.

THE SOVIET UNION IS SAVED

The victory acquired at the Battle of Stalingrad truly saved the Soviet Union from the brink of collapse at the end of 1942. The future of the Stalinist system was indeed played out on the banks of the Volga from August. This success finally eliminated any risk of collapse of the Russian economy by protecting the connection with the Caucasus, which carried out the transit of:

- British supplies;
- the oil supply of the Red Army.

Through this success, the Red Army also demonstrated its ability to conduct large-scale attacks. It was finally a match for the German army, which nevertheless remained superior in terms of its weapon quality.

A TURNING POINT IN WORLD WAR II

Consequences for the alliances of both sides

The alliances made by Germany unraveled after this defeat. The Romanians and the Italians that engaged alongside the *Wehrmacht* against the Soviet Union had also suffered heavy losses during the campaign. Under pressure from public opinion, they therefore focused on their national interests. The Italian leader Benito Mussolini (1883-1945) even asked permission to sign a separate peace agreement with the USSR. The Finns were also refusing to participate in any new offensive in Russia so as to be able to position their troops in a defensive position.

The victory of Stalingrad also had an impact on the Western allies of the Soviet Union. Since the Red Army was not defeated, the Russians could continue their fight against almost three quarters of the German armed forces. Given its importance, the British and the Americans later decided to involve Russia in important decisions about the war in Europe. Finally, the neutral countries such as Turkey were gradually turning to the Allies. Everything was falling apart for Nazi Germany.

A psychological turning point

Although no longer of any strategic interest, once the Volga had become impassable and the weapon factories were destroyed, the city of Stalingrad became a symbol in the fall of 1942. In both camps, populations were convinced by their leaders that the fate of the war was played out on the banks of the Volga. The stakes were indeed high: the Germans needed a victory; the Russians were not entitled to defeat.

In the Soviet Union and in occupied Europe, the German defeat raised a huge wave of hope. For the first time, the re-putation of the invincibility of the *Wehrmacht* was no more. The morale of all opponents of the Third Reich, at its lowest a few months earlier, had returned. After destroying an entire enemy army, the main beneficiaries of this renewed confidence were the Russian soldiers, whose fighting spirit and discipline improved.

The German population itself was surprised by the magnitude of the disaster. Confident in the superiority of its army and the genius of its leader, Germany saw its morale, hitherto unshakable, deeply affected. For the first time since taking office, part of the population blamed Adolf Hitler for the disaster. The Battle of Stalingrad thus marked the beginning of the break between the German people and its leader, whose mental health was beginning to waiver. The Germans gradually became aware that they were not invincible and began to doubt their final victory.

SUMMARY

1941
22nd June: Launch of Operation Barbarossa
Dec.: German troops are stopped
    at the gates of Moscow

1942
17th July: First combats in the
    surroundings of Stalingrad
23rd Aug.: Massive bombardment of the city
13th Sept.: German infantry attack on the city
19th Nov.: Soviet counter-attack
21st Nov.: Encirclement of the German army

1943
26th Jan.: Permission to capitulate
    is refused by the Fuhrer
31st Jan.: Rendering of
    Friedrich Wilhelm Ernst Paulus
2nd Feb.: End of the Battle of Stalingrad

- After the failure of the invasion of the USSR launched by the Germans in the summer of 1941, Adolf Hitler decided to launch a new offensive a year later, this time focused on the Caucasus and its oil fields to deal a fatal blow to the Soviet economy.

- Sorely weakened, the Soviet Union did not seem able to withstand another attack. Indeed, it had lost nearly two thirds of its grain production and the control of more than 30 million inhabitants, now under German occupation.

- The German plan was, starting from eastern Ukraine, to launch an army group in the south, to take the Caucasus, while the 6th Army, under the command of General Friedrich Wilhelm Ernst Paulus, headed towards the city of Stalingrad.
- The latter had formidable air support and 300 000 soldiers to take the city. The Russians had only 25 000 soldiers at the start of the battle. A German victory therefore seemed assured.
- After an intensive bombardment of the city, the German troops entered the outskirts of Stalingrad in early September.
- Under the command of General Vasily Ivanovich Chuikov, who implemented the *Rattenkrieg* tactics, a true art of close combat in urban areas, the Red Army managed to significantly slow the German advance.
- After two months of intense fighting, the Germans still did not manage to eliminate the Soviet resistance cores, which were refuelled at night by way of the river and were joined by 100 000 additional fighters.
- The Soviet counter-attack was launched at the beginning of November and allowed the Russians to encircle General Friedrich Wilhelm Ernst Paulus and his troops. Lacking in food and ammunition, the 6th Army had no choice but to surrender in February 1943.
- The losses for both sides were terrible, but the Soviets had forced a more powerful German army to surrender. This was a first since the beginning of the war. German supremacy in Europe slowly flickered, marking a major psychological turning point of the Second World War.

We want to hear from you!
Leave a comment on your online library
and share your favourite books on social media!

FIND OUT MORE

BIBLIOGRAPHY

- Beevor, A. (1998) *Stalingrad*. London: Viking.
- Corrigan, G. (2011) *The Second World War: A Military History*. London: Corvus.
- Gorodetsky, G. (2001) *Grand Delusion: Stalin and the German Invasion of Russia*. New Haven: Yale University Press.
- Hayward, J. (1998) *Stopped at Stalingrad: The Luftwaffe and Hitler's defeat in the East. 1942-1943*. Kansas: University Press of Kansas.
- Heiber, H. and Glantz, D.M. (eds.) (2004) *Hitler and His Generals: Military Conferences 1942-1945, From Stalingrad to Berlin*. New York: Enigma Books.
- Klee, E. (2003) Paulus. In *Das Personenlexikon zum Dritten Reich*. Frankfurt: Fischer Taschenbuch Verlage.
- Lopez, J. (2008) *Stalingrad. La bataille au bord du gouffre*. Paris: Economica.
- Montagnon, P. (2008) Paulus. In *Dictionnaire de la Seconde Guerre mondiale*. Paris: Pygmalion.
- Montagnon, P. (2008) Stalingrad. In *Dictionnaire de la Seconde Guerre mondiale*. Paris: Pygmalion.
- Montagnon, P. (2008) Tchouickov. In *Dictionnaire de la Seconde Guerre mondiale*. Paris: Pygmalion.
- Roberts, G. (2002) *Victory at Stalingrad: The Battle That Changed History*. London: Longman.
- Snyder, T. (2011) *Bloodlands. Europe Between Hitler and Stalin*. London: Vintage.

ADDITIONAL SOURCES

- Bastable, J. (2006) *Voices from Stalingrad: Nemesis on the Volga*. Cincinnati: David & Charles Ltd.
- Beevor, A. (2014) *The Second World War*. London: Weidenfeld & Nicolson.
- Craig, W. (2000) *Enemy at the Gates: The Battle for Stalingrad*. New York: Penguin.
- Erickson, J. and Dilks, D. (1998) *Barbarossa. The Axis and the Allies*. Edinburgh: Edinburgh University Press.
- Matthews, R. (2014) *Stalingrad: The Battle that Shattered Hitler's Dream of World Domination*. London: Arcturus.
- Müller, R.-D. and Uberschär, G.R. (1997) *Hitler's War in the East: A Critical Assessment*. Oxford: Berghan Books.

ICONOGRAPHIC SOURCES

- Stalingrad partly destroyed by German bombings. © German Federal Archives.
- German soldiers make their way through Stalingrad ruins. © German Federal Archives.
- Snipers entering a ruined house. © Russian Archives.
- Russian infantry in rubble of Stalingrad. © German Federal Archives.
- Surrender of Friedrich Wilhelm Ernst Paulus. Royalty-free reproduction picture.

FILMS AND DOCUMENTARIES

- *Stalingrad: Dogs, Do You Want to Live Forever?* (*Hunde, wollt ihr ewig leben*). (1959) [Film]. Frank Wisbar. Dir.

West Germany: Deutsche Film Hansa.

- *Lettres de Stalingrad.* (1969) [Film]. Gilles Katz. Dir. France: Pleins Feux.
- *Hot Snow.* (1972) [Film]. Gabriel Yegiazarov. Dir. USSR: Mosfilm.
- *They Fought for Their Country.* (1975) [Film]. Sergey Bondarchuk. USSR: Mosfilm.
- *Stalingrad.* (1989) [Film]. Yuri Ozerov. Dir. USSR/Czechoslovakia/East Germany/USA: Mosfil, Barrandov Studios, DEFA, Warner Bros. Pictures.
- *Stalingrad.* (1993) [Film]. Joseph Vilsmaier. Dir. Germany: Senator Film.
- *Enemy at the Gates.* (2001) [Film]. Jean-Jacques Annaud. Dir. USA: Paramount Pictures, Mandalay Pictures.
- *Stalingrad.* (2003) [Documentary]. Jörg Müellner and Sebastian Dehnhardt. Dir. Germany/Russia/Netherlands/Finland: Broadview TV.
- *Stalingrad.* (2013) [Film]. Fyodor Bondarchuk. Dir. Russia: Art Pictures Group, Non-Stop Production.

MUSEUMS AND COMMEMORATIVE BUILDINGS

- The Pavlov house, Volgograd (Russia).
- The Motherland stature on Mamayev Hill, Volgograd (Russia).
- The Museum of the Great Patriotic War, Kiev (Ukraine).
- The Panoramic Museum of the Battle of Stalingrad, Volgograd (Russia).

IMPROVE YOUR GENERAL KNOWLEDGE

IN A BLINK OF AN EYE !

www.50minutes.com

www.50minutes.com

Ebook EAN: 9782806275219

Paperback EAN: 9782806276629

Legal Deposit: D/2016/12603/57

Cover: © Primento

Digital conception by Primento, the digital partner of publishers.